W9-ARM-202

Life In The Forest

Written by Eileen Curran

Illustrated by Paul Harvey

Troll Associates

Library of Congress Cataloging in Publication Data

Curran, Eileen.
    Life in the forest.

     Summary: Introduces plants and animals of the forest
which the reader may find in the pictures.
     1. Forest ecology—Juvenile literature. [1. Forest
animals. 2. Forest plants] I. Harvey, Paul,
1926-   ill. II. Title.
QH86.C87   1985   574.5'2642   84-16455
ISBN 0-8167-0446-5 (lib. bdg.)
ISBN 0-8167-0447-3 (pbk.)

Copyright © 1985 by Troll Communications L.L.C.

All rights reserved. No part of this book may be used or
reproduced in any manner whatsoever without written permission
from the publisher.

Printed in the United States of America.

10 9 8 7 6

Who lives in the forest?

Look closely and
you will see.

5

What do you see?

Look quickly!
There goes a rabbit.

Did you look closely?
Did you see?

What grows in
the forest?

9

Look closely and you will see.
Up there! Look, an oak tree.

Here is a spruce tree

. . . and a pine tree.

13

Look over here!
Someone is eating berries.

Here are some wildflowers.

Did you look closely? Did you see?
Who lives on the forest floor?

Look closely and you will see.

Here is a ladybug.

Over there! Here is an ant.

Look quickly! There goes a snake.

Did you look closely?
Did you see?

Who else lives in the forest?
Look closely and you will see.

Here is a bear.

There goes a chipmunk.

25

Look closely and you will see.

What grows in the forest?

Who lives here?

The forest is a home for
many plants and animals.
What a wonderful place it can be!

Index